SECRET EQUINOX

Secret Equinox

Andrew K. Peterson

SPUYTEN DUYVIL

New York City

CONTENTS

for michele—

you are seen

written between the solstices
March 20 —June 21, 2022

*

To what purpose, April, do you return again?
Beauty is not enough.

—*Edna St. Vincent Millay*

SECRET EQUINOX

AUDACITY & ORACLE

Our task is to look at the world and see it whole.
Our task is to look at the world and see it
Our task is to look at the world
Our task is   the world
Our task is   the world
Our task is to look at the world and see
Our task

READING EDNA
after Edna St. Vincent Millay

How April comes
breezing in disorder
pacific bees spill
an idiot cascade
a pastel drivel
carries on about
The Spring Rebirth
Industrial Complex

my comments scan
as permit-parking-only
through a wine blizzard:
Who hurt you?
I love the US government
Heart heart breaking heart
Reading Edna
as I love an Irish Exit
willed rebellion
beaucoup nausea
juniper energy
peach reduction

fresh hole collapse
& Easter Monday's
half-off Peep's sale

Saint Malaise
yells *Rita!*
from a passing star
falling through currents
silky smooth city pop
I'm zoning out
in the dollar bin
passing winter-petaled
maggot brains
budding over
from the underworld

YOU MUST BELIEVE IN SPRING
after Bill Evans

must i ???
got the morbs

        breaking ritual
        with cordials

                elemental

                    essences

                frankincense, argan, myrrh
(… again with the myrrh?)
                  across cupid's kettle drum

                  "one morning i waked very early"

many thousands

gone without a song
the waking source

a mirrorlike coolness

OOOOOOOORRRRRRAAANNNNNNGGGEEEEE

pulls   across   the   surface   of   an orange

reversing form   &
function's

obsidian dance

          ashes rust

               sparks soak

the moon & miles davis
walk away from suicide watch

as solar soldiers
soldered to the shoulders of the sphinx

            "might we may"

               meet again
               head on

      nothing left   unopened
      nothing left   unsaid

MONO NO AWARE

A memory lives on the banks of another season, dies as flakes in the mouths of tellers (left unopened, nothing else is said). Commuting home from the bank, a man idles stranded on the highway for hours, sleeps in his car until he's rescued by patrol. Far away, in a little town in a little cape on a little hill, a woman waits by the hearth and keeps the fire warm. Asleep on the floor, she wakes to a drunk spinning in a snowbank, mistaking their driveway for the on-ramp. Flake by flake, a fine snow falling on the windowsill. A white cat watches the sky pelt the earth with its wicked dreams. The great blizzard catches on her tongue.

THE CAN
for Kevin Kilroy & Ben Hersey

to blossom
leave it all on crush
when i'm
a viral doormat
a leaky sleeve
& breeze-brush
fresh
hapappappy
(?)
as blue bottles
broken,
      leaking
all kinds
of kind
all varieties
      of can:

can & will
can do
can you?

street pets are friends
gonna wanna let 'em
follow us the way home
with their Feral-on-the-Niles
and their blue-fanged babies

grooves across poplars
of the popular grove

for us it's an ache
a chasm
for them it's okay
(maybe)

we'll glow in sway
as we sweep out
around the ashes
in the morning:

*the THe tHE theeeeeee tttttheee thhhhhe The tthee THE theeeee
caaaaaaan CAn Can cAN CaaaaaaaaN cananana can CaN CAN*

around
all kinds
of kind
all varieties
of sweet
      sweet
s-s-sweet
            can

dogwood blossoms
spill
up the mirror of
my crush

can
& will
can you ?
can do

LHOOQ
for Mona Lisa

by thief   by razor   by pebble by aggression's   naïve spray
paint by teacup   by mustache cake   in the name of
I've just seen a face   that could mean anything to any one
nation or whim   cheap money   in protest   for disability
access   citizenship denial   for climate agitation
thermic change   inaction   for yaya's ambiguous id
    ealizations   for pursed curves   plural invitation
for any revolt   any revolution   any gateaux reflects
a wry smile   a painted face   *enjoys*   but not *every*thing

HEX CODE

after Steve Carey

Any crocheting flunkies, cauliflower oligarchs of the oil brigade, any scandalized bridgers, any drunken groomsman half-emptied before the others notice he's a goner, any border-crossed gift taxers, razor-scootered sprinkler passers through, pilgrims of the safety vest, any brahmins tripping off the back porch, any splitters-up over de Tocqueville, any unrefined regimes, figgy googlers in red saguaro dresses, sprung break go-nowherers, backward portrait hangers of the hex codes, any self-cloning toxic worms invading Maine, any Robin Hood buskers of rogue Harvard knowledge, egg yolk blossom marketers hand in hand in sanitizing bloom, any vernal huskers of vengeance dreams, any beard farmers, any puke in my trauma pot, any portal dwellers in the silvery-purple flask effect, any Big Time Bogies, any psilocybin lovers in El Jardin de las Delicias, any sabbath stains in the pink garage, any conditional angels, is there anybody really alive out there?

MORNING CODEX
for Joanne Kyger

Rack focus from inbox to smiling tree swaying in outer breeze, envision beyond this mundane information to some kind of beautiful evidence. Anodyne messages imitate reflection: a wave of savings is coming my way! (Maybe.) Maybe the wave will find the way here, somewhere—where there's a moment, there's clarity—a causeway, or a crush course. This next sentence should be transitional summation of experience, a transformation from dull improv into blooming melt with a squeaky squeegee raked across the glass. Outside, leaves wave an auto-response to the power and pressure and the synch written into morning's subject codex. Fwd: You're Invited! to Our Feast of Eminent Impermanence.

HUMILITY
for Dom Centorino

it's late stage,
p e o p l e !
acting out
in glass houses
masking good
intentions, asking
crueler questions
thought better of
this year's
everything feels
crazy and wrecked
poor and wracked
joyously whack

sit in the mean a
while   quiet with
the antagonistic
mischievousness
of electric sound
the oscars myth

the great guts   hit
 like teenage summers
  when you vibed
    the pixies   felt
      the widescreen
        getting wider
            "your cards aren't the
            cleavage of this game"
          "billy, you fucker!"

    the weight
      of my empty head
        supported
          by the bend
            on an inward
                        elbow
          am i here, or
        just very near

MOBLEY ON THE CROSSTOWN
for Donald Vincent

morning's sleepy riddle
warms the work crowd
commuting back into
nothing so profound as
vibing off the Soul Station
from future destinations
back to here —
                    Split Feelin's
ring weary ears, the mind
                              kinks
            no explanation
unanswered calls
   pass fuchsia bright green lawn tiers
juiced perfume
                  strips the shine
from the moon blood's milk
                              ecliptic

A manbun sinks into the Amazon
book that cuts a body-chalk out
line against the cut-throat system

coldly closed we wake to,
                    daily, & endure:

The DOW in the plasma dumps
the Californian crust brakes
the Tops, the uterus, the middle
school, the church, parade attacks
seep deeper into broken haloes of
                    burnt ink

None-so graceful as lithe
bare shoulders' caramel
horripilation
            hipped to rising
                    heat
posture taut   as jaguar skin
wrapped against her throat
dips back into
            a dream of June
Jordan's strength to soften
the cross across this crosstown
drag-lit slice:

        If I Should Lose You
in "the resistance of simple daily

and nightly self-determination"
communing under nuptial crowns
bedazzled with weariness & hope
evidence sprayed across the slime
starry sinews by a work-a-day curl
uncured by paychecks . . . . .
. . . . or distance
I just don't know what I would do

Learn to
learn to draw
the line
back around the sun
from fortune's blues
to an unknown
destination's possibility

Dig Dis
I Remember
This I Dig of You

LAVA DREAM

we can really use *the rain*

i meant to say

we need *the rain*

then   i dreamt of lava

lava pouring down

the mountain

oozing

over arrows

lava by token proxy

lava over beets

over barrows

over wisps

and joints

chasms

alleys

over glitzy

rings, erudite hens

lava hie thee

lava goading moorings

lava over czars' armor

bowls of lava

putzing over

                    ey na and we
              sten and qi-qi
                    over ya fa
                          lava fumes gelling
                    over null id fur

              lava slow
          and peaceful
    lava from within
                burning over
                    every thing
                          i was unafraid
                                that's
                          the way
                    we set the steps
          and then we dance
                around
                the games we play
          for the rules we make   & disobey
                                & call
                    S U R V I V A L

          and then we dance around
          and then we dance around

RUSTIC OPENING

because
i'm going to die
there is no death

because
soon enough
i'll be dead
there is no death

because
i'll be born again
there is no death

o o a w h h

because
the afterlife loves you
infinity plus infinity
plus infinity

because infinity is
one plus one
plus two
plus one

AFTERLIFE, OR THE LOTUS

The richest man on Earth orders employees
return to office jobs by Tweeting from outer space

A blooming lotus flower simultaneously
carries seeds inside itself while it blooms

Pregnant woman becomes pregnant while
already pregnant; pregnantly gives birth to triplets

In Massachusetts, the most commonly searched
word spelling is the word... *Massachusetts*

What's the color of karma? Mid-neutral sage
with avocado undertone (Perfect for a bedroom accent)

I don't trust old souls. Why haven't you escaped samsara yet?

M.B.T.A. Update: Live updates are temporarily unavailable

EASTER IN BABEL

buttoned to the gold
anchors in heavy blue
wool   allergenic   in heat
i kneel, mouth an un
familiar prayer
mingle with the flow
ers sewn to cloches
& fascinators unlike
looser pleas passed
through the blood-
stained fingerprints
pressed above
my bed to bless
the souls of those i
love who live, the ones
who don't, and still we
love thee too
     closer
clouds pluck abstract
harps or so i'm told
or so i'm bold to build
temples in my mind

where violet flags fly
above the pride
i parachute down
with a three-legged hound
strapped between my legs
squeeze too tight

he'll bite i'll loosen
we'll fall into the flames
translucent ocean green
tower-displaced thresholds
aloe-smear of wax & fats
so into dawn we lower
gentle in teutonic bloom
arrow the clearway
to calm the hound
to calm the hound within
as below,
            so above
and i don't know his name

XANTHIUM PARACHUTE

you are everywhere
with every heartbeat

painting the river
that runs through
all three worlds:

the quiet passion

the talented maple

cocklebur and bull

*

to shed tears

to shed the past

to shed skin

to shed leaves

to shed water like a duck

to shed the blood of thine enemy

to shed thy Light on me!

*

you are everywhere
with every heartbeat
roaring of an ocean

: the roll of distant thunder

: the sound of a conch shell

: the sound of a bell

  to a being being rung

Equinox — First Sign of Spring — Spring Succeeds — Spring Is Here — Up Jumped Spring — Joy Spring — Silver Springs — Spring Is Here — Springs-ville! — Another Spring — Botticelli Spring — Can't Stop The Spring — A Fine Spring Morning — They Say It's Spring — It Might As Well Be Spring — Spring Among The Living — I Live In The Spring — Spring Hall Convert — Dusty Springfield — Bruce Springsteen & The E Street Band — Filipino Box Spring Hog — Springtime Can Really Hang You Up the Most — Springtime Can Kill You — You Must Believe In Spring — Equinox

SPRING, AN ÉTUDE

Sprung of the leaf
it takes the role
of causal beginning
with cause to rise
as origin, as is berth
to still — announce
suddenly — release
from sunrise wax
tides sprouting beards
or public hearts
when plants begin
to bud, the source,
the day, lengthening
conscious of words
—*carbuncle, pustule* —
            or of nothing;
to see the full worth –

                        to shine

spri  gs
viole t
grow th

GIANT STEPS
after John Coltrane

would've been
May   creating
for practice
write
by learning to
remember you by
vague expression-
sounds
a secret adhesive
sensible, windable
singable as
                  Duke

in private aspects
of a manner:
cool over-tones
so   over blues
or keeping it
simple
starting again:

could've been May
may've been
                spiral
in a heavyweight
countdown
dramatic progression

tiny
rippling
harmonics
in the key of
keyless centers
or giant like
GIANT STEPS

rippling
'til the clouds roll by

DECISION

after Sonny Rollins

a kiss on your
novocain mouth
little abrupt blocks
wander on the changes

trees from branches —
these tender senses —
it's apparent the hawk
surprised the speaker:

a breakdown
with transparent tone
crackle of a naked flame's
opaque swaggeroso

baby
i got rhythm
with a honeysuckle bridge

extras echo from before
could you feel a thing

IN SOLIDARITY, AFTER A PARTY
after Frank O'Hara

I don't always know what you're feeling
still, I love you for what you keep
inside your protective bedside blue
dragon, that spring-into-action kiss
lobbed in my direction as I sit
                    maudlin in the heatwave

                                        , & then it's on
me to pick up on or misinterpret realizations.
                                What game
                                shall I learn today?

The things I wish I said
                        to siblings' casual racism
when they can't get a table at the country club:

"You may've moved to Jupiter,
your head's still in Uranus"

 &, opposite like static, pose
together over blossom frosting
clings to widescreen plasma

lining up another shot
cleats on a faraway green

    "The tiny divine
    part of me is greater
    than my human guilt."

    If I listen to *Unity*
    Softly
        as in Morning Sunrise

    Maybe
    spilled Prosecco down your shirt
    dries the same as tears

            in solidarity.
    Our love knowledge
    another étude for ways to re-begin.
    Sour rings
        freshen in the tide.

THERE SHE GOES AGAIN

Rhythmic
plastic slap
of dry clean

bag, arm
pitted from
sped-by bike

hastens
Becca down
Blanche—

hair fixed
to wind-
smoothed

afters, the ir-
resolute skirt
stains the work

of chemicals'
fizzed out
Promises.

BLADE RUNNER LOVE THEME
after Vangelis

Knowing
his second name:
Odysseus

means he begins
his long journey
in the roads of fire

from there he'll
send his chariot-
stretched notes

Juno to Jupiter
make dreams last
longer than the night

INSPECTION OF THE MIND IN JUNE
after Philip Whalen

got the morbs
not up to dick
tight as a boiled owl

a sunflower head-dial
spirals out of my nose

as intoxicated bees
simmer in the hum of honey

12 / VI / 2022

ALLERGY

i fight last
night in the
dream fight
the writing by
a poem i forget
this morning
i apologize
to morning
i reach for
the writing in
in the dream
i remember:
(eyes water
what they
inhale, sneeze
a hem-fresh batch
of rococo confetti:
sarcasm
pronounced
s o u r   chasm   )
mornings
in the mouth
the beast
of an eyelash coast

i sleep with
Dream Queen
spinning
on the platter
soft hugs
for delicate flowers
still smell like
yesterday's sun

A RED WHEEL

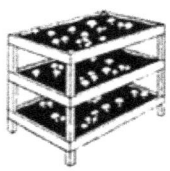

---

to predict the future

a curve is to carry out

a certain operation

on its past

(I want to do what nature doesn't do)

———————————

for being human
the signs
escape you

somebody else's horizon

———————————

Tacoma...Emporia
... Tuscahoma ... Roanoke ... Daytonsburgh ...
Baltimore ... Philadelphia ... Williamsburg ... Buffalo
... Dover ... New Brunswick ...

Apple ... Potato ... Watermelon ...

any difference which makes a difference

---

i.e. "Ho Chi Minh's daughter"

CHECK HERE IF NO CHANGES

_____

check box erroneously

checked

The answer is

_____

pieces of a picture

light in the corner of the eye

THE GILDED PALACE OF SIN

Sneaky Pete wears a baggy midnight blue
sweatsuit: the dumbest yellow pterodactyl
swoops across rhinestone sprinkle-distant
star-cry. Chris Hillman wears a lush cobalt
double peacock suit, chilled glitter branch drops
topaz coral breaks from pleat to pleat, a black silk
western bow tied to a light-blue pointed collar.
Chris Etheridge wears an Edwardian frock coat
covered in classic red and yellow roses, pink ruffles
spill through the bouquet overdose.
Gram Parsons' white cavalry twill is embroidered
with naked ladies, rhinestone-studded pot leaves,
sequin-dotted poppies, capsule and sugar cube sleeves.
Flames lick bell-bottoms, a gleaming "t" stretched
across his back. Suzanne and Bridget stand in the splinter-
ringed shack frame, in maroon and grey depression
era dresses, looking distantly removed and cool.
How awkwardly they withstand the glittering Nudies
adorn the cosmic desert where they've never been
before, may not return to again—this Age of Aquarius
on the sixth of February in the year of our dark lord 1969.

CHAR VIV

after Pierre Reverdy

your déjà vu voice
failed duller missions

as the death of love
drips from a high
latrine's black ceiling

tears sizzle on the sun-floor
detached light
surer at the core:

the right hand's
putting on the left
like a lover's rainbow

silver-gold exaltations
bowling through smoke
empty of sorrow

full of pluming flail
lit across stolen grain

baked listlessly in
a harvestless
bliss-setting breeze

a harmonizing sun-tide
the sea responds with torque
a concert-dance bliss
a two-headed freap
the mind's perfume sighs

atmosphere! atmosphere!
i'll remember your voice
to the bella donna of cathedrals

(slumlords,
keep practicing
on the pillars of the universe)

two groundless apéritifs
s'il vous plait

guess i just love
to love; to
love, i love,
and
     do

HEAD SOUP
after Alfred Jarry

Orchestrated madness
demands countermelodic mendacity

: Re-collective Orchestra
& The Debbie Allen Dance Academy
Perform "Starburst"
Live from the Hollywood Bowl

Interruptions, new continuities
to slaughter the charmless
indiscreet oligarchic bourgeoisie

: Pere Ubu serves Putin
head soup
made of radioactive wind
blown thru Ukrainian wheat

The banquet years —an empty plate

: Seven Keys for Seven Doors
To Seek a New Home
by Brother Jack McDuff

THE STRAWBERRY MOON
DONNA SUMMER DISCO PARTY
for a coworker

tsssk. I had no other plans just plain plum dog forgot
the delicate strawberries
                froze in the fridge
thawed on the counter rot in blue fiesta
       & carelessly tossed in the bin
                mushy purple shadows
       hurtle sideways against the canyon wall
   up over the ridged lip and out
      into milk-black inner space

Reed retrieves the menu from the desk then returns dutifully
to filing:
       "I just want to get umm.... wings"
         Mmm, there are seeds
   within these structures of perception
  between memory &
         the mightiness it takes to grow

I had no other plans just plain plum forgot
The Strawberry Moon Donna Summer Disco Party:
She works hard for the money
           so you better
               treat her right

NOTES FOR A FUTUREPOEM
after DeWitt Godfrey / for Jack Collom

Remember
the feral phoebe
skitterssssss cross
Godfrey's rusty ovoids
q-u-a-a-k-k-k-k-k-k-e

Remember
scene's reduced scope
shld lead
irredeemably
to nest-hood
feedback patterns
affirmatively
activating
unconscious
sun loops
of inter-dimensionality...

Remember
yarn-spun
cacophonies

Collomesque
sub-loops:
Remember
I
get very confused
(that's called
A Day's Work)

y o d e l a y h e e h o o o
y o d e l a y h e e h o o o
y o d e l a y h e e h o o o
o d e l a y h e e h o o o
e l a y h e e h o o o
l a y h e e h o o o
a y h e e h o o o
a y h e e h o o o
a y h e e h o o o

Remember
the feral phoebe
crushin' on
K A B L O O E Y

SECRET EQUINOX
for Chan Marshall

between ruminant targets
and the hunger under surfers

between dry Sentinel bitterroot and
the arsonist's smoking phonebook

between pyrotechnic roses
and a paraphrased adaptation

between the claw hammer stomp
and the buffalo mercy highway

between midnight's bon-bon
and dawn's eponymous silence

between exploding galaxies
and diminuendo hairpins

between bluebird dust
and a psalm-sharpened blur

between the disrobing waif
and His nimbus-soldered skull

between a loosened cloudburst
and centerless glitter ripples

between the torn clock's veil and
sleep's counterclockwise blinker

between the picker and the dancing
and the elders and the good times

between boredom's crease
and reaching inspiration's limit

between turbulent landscapes
and morning's homesick blue

between the Spanish Civil War
and a Silvertone Sears guitar

between amending darkness
and equity and balance

between flowering hibiscus
and hibiscus shadow lands

between the secret equinox and
these unsummoned thresholds

between you and I is we
and what we keep
between us is the world

between the fold in the page
and the word in the fold

and the shadow on the word
and the shadow on the fold

and the fold in the shadow
and the world in the fold

and the shadow of the ground
on the ground

THE GREATEST
after We Are King

under my bare feet
another spring gone past, un-
conscious, undefea-*THUD!*

A wounded monarch crash-lands
struggling to regain flight under the weight
of its human-size costume wings,
upending the last haiku of the season
with the ambition and amplitude of its greatness…

through my heart
it beats like crazy
someone's got to fall
into the
timeless
spread
across
the sky
of an
instant's
blossom
moment

NOTES

Reading Edna —Inspired by Edna St. Vincent Mallay's Spring-hating poem "Spring."

Audacity & Oracle —The title is a pun on the title of The Zombies' classic psychedelic pop album *Odessey & Oracle*.

The texts of this poem, *Xanthium Parachute* and *Rustic Opening* are found language from *The Next Whole Earth Catalog*.

You Must Believe in Spring —Title is borrowed from a song title written by Michel Legrand and Jacques Demy, and the poem is somewhat inspired by pianist Bill Evans.

"Solar soldier soldered to the shoulder of the sphinx" —Some Egyptologists believe there's a solar alignment between the Sun and the Sphinx which happens during the Spring Equinox.

Mono No Aware —"the pathos of things", also translated as "an empathy toward things", or "a sensitivity to ephemera". A Japanese idiom for the awareness of impermanence, or transience of things, and both a transient gentle sadness (or wistfulness) at their passing as well as a longer, deeper gentle sadness about this state being the reality of life.

The Can —Inspired by a sound project by friends Ben Hersey and Kevin Kilroy. Each took one side of a cassette tape, speaking a single word in variations for the duration of the side. Side A: Kevin: the word "the". I think he recorded in a single take locked in a bathroom with a recorder. Side B: Ben: the word "can", recorded in numerous takes.

"Sweet can": Reference to *The Simpsons'* episode "Homer Badman".

LHOOQ —Inspired by the occasion of the vandalism of Leonardo da Vinci's Mona Lisa by a cake-throwing climate change protester at The Louvre in May. Poem borrows language from a 1963 article on Mona Lisa defacement by Salvador Dali, and a 2019 commentary on Dali's essay by da Vinci biographer Martin Kemp in ARTnews. The title LHOOQ is also the title of Marcel Duchamp's Mona Lisa Dadaist piece.

"Enjoys but not everything" —Line from "Juan Ramón Jiménez: The Landscape of the Soul" by Rachel Frank.

"Is there anybody really alive out there?" —Often asked by Bruce Springsteen to his audience during live performances.

Morning Codex —The phrases "beautiful evidence" and "envisioning information" are also book titles by statistician and political scientist Edward Tufte.

The lines "The protagonist of electric sound, the Oscars, the myth, and the great hits" and much of *Blade Runner Love Theme* are adapted from Greek Prime Minister Kyriakos Mitsotakis' statement in response to the passing of Greek New Age musician Vangelis.

Inspection of the Mind in June —The poem contains antiquated Victorian slang terms: got the morbs —temporary sadness; not up to dick —unwell; tight as a boiled owl —slightly drunk.

Mobley on the Crosstown —Written during bus commute while listening to saxophonist Hank Mobley's classic Blue Note album *Soul Station*. Poem includes the album's song titles.

Spring, an Étude —Contains phrases from an etymological dictionary entry for the word "spring". "The tiny divine part of me is greater than my human guilt" —Clarice Lispector.

Decision —Some vocabulary is taken from the liner notes to Sonny Rollins' *Volume 1* (Blue Note Records), Freddie Hubbard's *Live at Studio 104* (WeWantSounds), and song titles on Anthony Williams' Blue Note album, *Spring*.

Rustic Opening —"one plus one plus two plus one" is confused dialogue from *Clue: The Movie*.

Afterlife, or The Lotus —Collage of recent news headings and Google searches.

Lava Dream —Combination of a dream, with words from a game of Scrabble I played with Michele the night before the dream.

Red Wheel —"I want to do what nature doesn't do." is a quote from Philip Guston's interview with Clark Coolidge in *I Paint What I Want to See* (Penguin UK, 2022). "For being human / the signs escape you" is a quote from Jack Spicer's "A Red Wheelbarrow". Other content is taken from *The Next Whole Earth Catalog*.

Char Viv —A somewhat homophonic translation of Pierre Reverdy's poem "Chair Vive" (which translates as "Live Flesh").

The Strawberry Moon Donna Summer Disco Party —Boston hosts an annual dance party to celebrate the life and music of Donna Summer (born in Dorchester neighborhood of Boston). One phrase adapts a quote from an abstract for Roger Brooke's article "Merleau-Ponty's Conception of the Unconscious": "The unconscious is situated as an ambiguous, lived consciousness within the structure of perception, founded on the forgotten body's world-relations." Published in *South African Journal of Psychology*, Dec. 1986.

Notes for a Futurepoem —The poem references sculpture artist DeWitt Godfrey's art installation *Quake*, located in the bird-heavy bike/pedestrian path in Cambridge, MA. "crushin' on kablooey" —from an interview with Kurt Vile.

Secret Equinox —Integrates language from: a critical review of my poetry book *Good Game* written by Gregory Wolos on Doug Holder's Boston Area Small Press and Poetry Scene Blog from October 2020; *I Paint What I Want to See*, Interviews and Lectures by painter Philip Guston (Penguin Classics, 2022); descriptions of the number Five in the Tarot Deck (keen.com); and Erin Osmon's book-length exploration of John Prine's self-titled debut album (Bloomsbury Academic's 33 1/3 Series, 2022).

The Greatest —"though my heart, it beats like crazy / and someone's got to fall" are lyrics to the song "The Greatest" by We Are King from their self-titled debut album (released 2016 by King Creative).

ACKNOWLEDGMENTS

Many thanks to the editors of the small lit journals who published some of these poems in earlier versions: Geoffrey Gatza at *BlazeVOX Journal*; Mark Young at *Otoliths*; Suzanne Mercury at *Boog City*; Jeffrey Side at *The Argotist*; Isobel O'Hare and Carleen Tibbets at *Dream Pop Journal*: William Allegrezza at *Moss Trill*; and Keifer Logan at *Where Is the River*.

Special editorial thanks to t thilleman at Spuyten Duyvil for your genius attention to detail, and ongoing support of my writing.

All love to my friends and family; especially to Jared Hayes for your beautiful letter and inspiring friendship; and to michele lubowsky for your fearless loving and partnership.

Kygers and Whalens to all.

www.ingramcontent.com/pod-product-compliance
Lightning Source LLC
Chambersburg PA
CBHW051622120626

46551CB00014B/1909

SCORPIO JOURNAL

Scorpio Journal

Andrew K. Peterson

Spuyten Duyvil

New York City

Secret Equinox/Scorpio Journal
Copyright (c) 2023 by Andrew K. Peterson
ISBN 978-1-959556-60-2

Published by Spuyten Duyvil
spuytenduyvil.net

Front Covers and Gallery by Andrew K. Peterson
Book Design by T. Thilleman

 Library of Congress Control Number: 2023942889

CONTENTS

SCORPIO JOURNAL
23 oct— 21 nov / xxi

Welcome to Scorpio season! Remember who the F you are! Refuse toxic behavior! Make moody playlists! Do sexy brooding! Wear all black everything! Witches! Cast spells for healing! Make magic and emotional mayhem! Life is short! Death is inevitable! Risk everything for joy!

Chani Nicholas

OCTOBER 23

does change buoy
the atonal
warble
that contains
deep fever
woe in tonic
rumble
sides with oblivion
glides along
a ridged heart's
harvest
water-moon
of pale blue
stationery?

syncopating colors, the game slips between clouds,
the coordinated crowd turns together, waves
to the looming building over the sold-out stadium.
behind reflective windows of the children's hospital,
little hands wave back. cut to ads for swilling

yesterday's coffee
porter on my breath
autumn's sharpened sky
a melancholic open splice

IN ALL BLACK

"All we need is a tragic universe."

Life's a short fuse
for too much else
besides anything
outside itself:
emotional mayhem

Anselmic disclosure
self-effacing demon
meander   deeper
than mere truth
telling   so return

this nostalgia-worn
adhesive to the
envelope of bone
& bury (or exhume?
can't tell the shovel

its direction) in
the older-not-wiser
country
in all black everything
i.e. the Italians
and their fine asses

Pleasure's a fish
& i'm a water sign

so says
The Butterfly

if necessary
(as game 7's
unnecessary)

nevertheless
"risk everything for joy"

The Butterfly
says so

VIDEO VOICE

after Jasmine Dreame Wagner

Every Friday they drop the white horse neck-deep into the Swamp of Sadness. Atrayu (stand-in for the reader, stand-in for the viewer) screams *Atax!* screams yanking at the reins *Atax!* suck in the sucking suck at the neck *Atax!* as the horse's nostrils fill with mud. They fucking drown the white horse in the Swamp of Sadness controlled by the deepening powers of this never-ending sorrow. I sob at the Video Voice, ask my mother to rent it again and again. Today I walk the muddy streets with that perfumed memory: crinkled videotape mixed with vacuum dust and tapehead cleaner. Skimpy pines and tempestrarii in the median are all that's left of the laguna. They drown the white horse...

A WHALENESQUE
for Suzanne Mercury

Have Sumatran fishing crews found the fabled Island of Gold?

Dramatic periods of social personal emotional political upheaval
: to walk across the graffiti footbridge carrying a full-length mirror

    Keep Your Soul Together

            Love will Find a Way

      A Love Supreme

    Smiley Smile

"It will be as much an improvement over Sounds
as that was over Summer Days."

      Your connection is not private

GRAVEYARD SMASH

Let's do The Time Warp
The Monster Mash
commute   thru a deluge to
Cantabrigian doom-work

devour

                pumpkins
drizzled, slightly
ditzy, zazzle
the golden populous
reeling thru the yellow
leaking thru the red
& slightly fuzzed

what's better
than one fall train?
two? the fall of
capital w/syncopated
bus schedules?

Let's do the time warp

                again
ha-ha   there you go

NOR'EASTER

the headache barometric
who owns the air rights?

poured from
a cooler to
the gutter
down across
the pike
mauves
over mass

i think
of Michael
Koshkin

cinematography's
natural graduation
from Milton
Parade Rain

          & Logan's small-town
          label gone garage
          minor consolations?

     how to capture
     umbrellas
     in the midst
& how the Charles flows
inland from the sea

          Take it from
          The Vikings
          who bury
          their beloveds'
          bodies in boats

"& the sea is a bedtime story"

"to satisfy beyond advantage"

Tide me over
til next time
with all of it   always

JAZZ IS DEAD

"there're no do-overs
it's all just murder birds"

caffeine eyeballs
dip in golden disco
donut massage

sun-reflective
rainshine
morning corners
disappear in

finely-tuned
wind curves
of synchronized vibrations
pulse deep
within the mix

this piece at
this time in
this place—

"inspiring beauty
& respect (but jazz is dead)
...are we being our best?"

OCTOBER 27

& then, in one morning
            rumbles "the director"
                        of commercial construction

waving plastic bag
            w/ Mickey Mouse mask
                        for the office costume contest

karl & i
            telepath premortem
                        in the presence of madness,
                                    bitten
                                    cheek plucks

loose the tongued polka
            dotted masque, exhausted
                        from this too oft-worn

defense built back
            better behind
                        the pageant's
                                    tragic kingdom

& this is all mind,

       mind you, & silly me

              without a crane

to lift, settle,

      welcome one

         M-I-C-

             K-E-Y

        M-O-U-

             S-E

               as welcomed one can

      be

TURNER CLASSIC

crazed fruit   sigh, i mean
lake-cupped celluloid hands
water-skiing & muted lust's
sightless signs   the young

couple necking in the pines
hesitation's stooped hip-shy
skill in familiar buttoned closeup:
feet, their silent musicality

for navigation
"chromatically,
 the structure unfolds"

(fade-out)
      breath-like

            motionless

ONCE WAS RIMA

boisterous
coitus copious
uninterruptus

ursula the populous
sea creature fair
rima the jungle girl
phaedra-red

"in either the sensuous or
the metaphysical dimension"

you wake feeling
worry & hope
that hope doesn't
talk in its sleep

kiss me good
morning happy
halloween, your love

my love remembers
the best advice to take —
what once was rima
don't forget to shake

Bernadette visits in dream to ask what i'm afraid of: abandonment, acceptance, emptiness, imposter syndrome, death of loved ones, people hating my poems (do they hate me?), a nail in the throat, war, not so much claustrophobia but being confined with others (elevators, trolley), the great nothing approaching while being trapped in shopping cart (recurring childhood dream), waking frozen with boogers for eyes, lungless outer space, oceanic canyons' deep recesses, random violence, incessant pain, losing teeth, never being alone, the witch monster behind the dumpster in *Mulholland Drive*, failure, public ridicule, being misunderstood, brain bacteria, the word and the meaning and the color beige, extended metaphor, street solicitors, asking for help, small talk, losing the drive to create & express love & gratitude, forgetting that to breathe is to pause is to understand deeply

RECOVERING THE JEWEL
FROM DRAGON PALACE

Erasure for Peter Orlovsky
whose Dharma name is
"Ocean of Generosity"

bound to sacred
sense, a self-supporting
tradition: women
weathering countless
storms of time
> *passed deeper down*

>> *into deeper origin*
>> *perennial mermaids*
>> *scour ocean floor*
>> *in search of pearls*
>> *precious shellfish*
>>> *seaweed, abalone*

>>> *in imperial waves'*
>>> *crash dragon guards*
>>> *fight creatures*
>>> *with only the blade*
>>>> *of identity's core*

wearing only
stitched fabric
in simplicity
loincloth, headscarf
collecting waves
        warm & graceful

                    naturalness,
                    visual acuity,
                    lung capacity,
                    instincts
                    of a hunter
                        to ward off evil

                                gasp exhaling
                                shore-pitched
                                whistles
                                the final breath
                                to embolden &
                                protect
                                before the next
                                    plunge

UNTITLED

'81, two or so
i play with fire
engine matches turn
around box-sprung weaves
perpetual race to invisible
return. come down
stairs,
      andrew, &
              meet someone...
step of my step-
father in the shadow
of dad's easy wingback.

i spit in his face,
he spits back.
back up the engine

into the fire weave.
let's play who's sorrier.
i'm always first to apologies

POW RAWR

Ugly memories
mixed with alumin
um breeze & western
sounds struck to
the razorface fence

Assaulted w/edges
after later i'll spill out
sparks from the lock
hard to beat an opening
without an alibi

The rupturing sup
ercontinents, interp
enetrate underfoot
, colossal teth
ered dripping adren

aline that tastes like
fear, bad decisions
decadence entar
decendo en saudade
Pangaea sinus rift

Agharta face
sounds familiar
flame-cleaned
by a moth
just like you

just like you

RAW DAEMON ALCHEMY

with deep shame
i've yet to learn
what's a synonym for

        what number to start the count
        to pull the cosmic fang
        & unwind this myth of stars

        counting backwards
        add cilantro to
        the violent health safari

here for the bridges and glitter

the humane divinity of autumn

creatures who don't pad quietly

with a jolly collide of molecules

another fatty bungler
slips away from peace
chickadeedeedee
bob would s/w/ay

DEVIL'S NIGHT
i.m. Daniel Dumile

new cats
pet old hands
& wholly smoked
90s cloves
stay smoked
in abandoned
90s buildings'
burning lungspell
unseen within
telepathic storms
peach pit misses
radiate across
inner-space
to friends' faces
cross a mountain
sun table
roll dope memories
& save the fireflies
braided to a path
inside the volcano
there's a heart

that can't be rained on
when the beat is
my mood, doom
is my bell
bell is my beat
beat is my doom bell too

NOVEMBER 1

eleven o'clock
daylight's acorn
plops on hairy head

good luck in some
ancient iconography
"you can't force

something to be your
truth" held too close:
these attachments

(i should learn from trees)
kerplunk
so goes my faith in silence

TREE LAWS

"How much beauty has rolled off the breast of a dying swan?"
(Orlovsky said that)

how much grace shredded by antlers of the cosmic moose?

how much soul protected from the trophy hide of a grizzly mama?

how many confessions leap into eyes of an indifferent monk?

"Under Massachusetts' Fallen Tree Law wherever the tree landed,
that person is responsible for dealing with it, regardless of where
the tree came from."

how many trees fallen into the heart of the solitary moon drinker?

"VALENTINE AND PEARL"

Valentine and Pearl
in formerly The Port

Titian chestnut
pine-moss rot
autumn's somnolence
maroon in ochre
groves & gold-brown
gloom, rhododendrons'
dry tetraponic
blue, porch lunch
& husky russet,
flannel, dying ivy
giving bloom to
passed out chloroform
on a scumbag's lawn

How come you're not movin', Murph?
He goes, what did I just tell *you?*

Aparajita

DOUBLE RAINBOW

Heartbreak is behind him but hope is always just ahead, a pin-light through the clouds in the shape of a mythological figure known only as "babe".

It's not enn-you
or even enn-i
it's *ennui,* babe—
please remember me
to your heart.

After hollow's rain
comes matriculating*
our worried-well off-brand
sense of horror show.

*Note to self: stay
skeptical transmogrifying
subtlety into spiritual verbs:

companioning, guiding, uncovering, listening, forming.

The imperceivable arc breaks
sharp, apocryphally, with light.
You will forget the world, but remember the feel.

NOVEMBER 2 ½

i have charming dreams;
reunions & readings
listen in on poet friends
still my teachers. wake
a guitar pic in my hair
: what songs have I been?

i remember the first class on literary remixes (King Lear plus
Moo equals   et cetera), baffled at synchronicities— Judy
Garland and the Dark Side— skeptical, then convinced in
the gorgons. For my final term paper: a mixtape: one side
with songs i dug: Scratch Perry's heavy-lidded dub, Mor-
phine's *Cure for Pain*, "E-bow the Letter", prob some *OK
Computer*; the other with songs my mother chose: Here
Comes the Sun; This Is Your Song; Don't You Make My
Brown Eyes Blue.

POEM FOR MY GRANDFATHER
ON THE OCCASION OF ABBA'S
FIRST ALBUM RELEASED IN 40 YEARS

Kiss me I'm Swedish too
another maiden voyage
hands clasp
behind the nebula
(I mean vertex)
in surrender to
Dancing Queen-quiet
another mind
within itself
I can't read
/ you wouldn't tell

You had Gold in your tapes
temporary shelter for the brides
widowed to war memories
crayons and paper for our visits
money in the breadbox

The men in my life keep their secrets
sad that I've learned from
(stolen)

which one of us was costume?

Goya's Red Boy
his leashed magpie
stalked by wide-eye cats
beneath a convex mirror

Can you hear the drums?
Can you hear the drums, Fernando?

Simple franks & beans & kettle chips
served on paper plates for supper

DEAD PHILOSOPHER
after Laura Theobald

You have a crush on a dead philosopher. With your crush comes the responsibility that will help lift the grease-smeared lid. Their compliments are an impossible meatball balanced on the z-axis of erased blue leaves. Their whispers flicker like an *onodes martenot* thrown from an overpass onto the live wires which empower it. Their handholds lacking in content nevertheless are recognizable as the stain of autobiography. Their embrace a consolidation of transfused amnesias from apple cheeks to country tweed. Each French kiss leads to grey orgasm, with its duty to be remembered, and its right to be forgotten. In their rotting eyes, ghosts panhandle your beautiful evidence, which will be stolen and published under their name in fresh soil. Brushing blue leaves from the catacombs, you're unsurprised the middle name carved on their stone reads Memory.

SCORPIUS (MYTH)

"i'm all slaughter
every mammal
in this motherfucker"

orion &
scorpion banished
deep into punk

nova suburbs to curb
excessive mortal pride
(post trash-talk hook

    & sting)
typical scorpius   stay
far away, but close

are they my forces
or the forces i'm within?

being made of stars
& heart, room & tail—
the cat's paw nebula

SLOW DANCE

going
through
motion's
paired
measures:

mind
design
matter
communicates
abundance,
rare
pleasure

good night everone
marijhuana

"it's only life
waveing to its self"

NOVEMBER 6

marches and matches
a being floating
through the throat
chest shuffles into spark

finish the water
before refilling the glass

o ye runcible utterable
a day be done
                    awake

•

i want something
more portable
so much so until
i stop carrying
anything at all

cos it doesn't fit
this grasp any more
no small accident
this learning to let—
keep re-minding me

•

don't want to get old   but grow. not by
            getting that wisdom wrong

the most complex hybrid strains
= simplest grains
= need the least adjustment

with that, she makes the bed around me

•

            on beacon
horns lock up morning light
honk   if you know we're just guests
guests of Pawtucket
guests of Massa-adchu-es-ets
and   of here

•

Empire Beauty School

sunny commons   weeping
willow shadows lip the swan pond

there's no angry way to say
B U B B L E S

KING TIDE

how to change: the changes feign
every chorus
every rise
every brackish harbor droplet spilled across
long wharf, the stench of rotten
                                    kings
every atm kiosk scent: my father's cologne
misunderstanding childhood in abstract
weekend arcs thru rocky coast's new beaches
lacking love but for another— obligation
to the creature they made, burning
3 black Buick engines, fumes
across state lines on daily loan
melting glaciers to protect income tax
lay the overheating planet's doomed fate
at the velcro'd feet of children of divorce
who sleep the long waves home
missing autumn's rotting vein
ambers   auburns   burgundies
the dream of rot & rift
the dream of generous kings

LA NOTE BLEUE

the heart sets over sunburnt water rhythms
crossing patterns   99.9% without resistance
not wistful, not sentimental, just missing
out being on one's way, dreaming among
sensations, impressions, meditations
blaze the underwood from here on out
hopped citrus strewn across dull green
mustard pall of spotted brown
la note bleue   dancing in the check out
weaving fabrics within   cracks & wriggles
open a single yellow football-shaped leaf
a nuance of hours & phases change makes:
Remember the fate of the early worm

Nov 9th
42'd birthday poem
& in memory of Lewis Warsh

TRY TO TRY

Try to try to catch
this vintage MTV
multiple Timberlakes
dance contra neon
the sirens want
to be the ones
to be so quick
to rock my body,
walk away
in a pivoting pepper
couch-cool indica
flame-wheel body
to another siren's
redemption sting
refilling night's
body whirl-
pools pink fangs
& glitter flickers
off shifting corners
Trying
    (Trying)
for the joy
is in the giving

STING CATALOGUE

for no wonder's
a self-extinguishing
golden bell \ chilly
morning wicks \

nautical buttons
\ a blue noble
eucalyptus \
arranged in wooden boxes

it's really nice
to see the world
celebrate something—

destroy
to create. solid adobe
and deep, deep wine

is pocket pocket
inside? and comfort
— and wrinkle or pill
for warmth

looking for cuts
slimmed through
gum in dark wash
resilient
past season

a fluid knot
in honeycomb

brushed soft
impacts
like a stretch
i needed

BUS RIDE

How to tell
this is track two
is that there's
three-eyed dog-
glyph— red &
yellow flames
diamond collar
to a Roman clef
carved "II" in
center-spoke
track title:
"BUS RIDE"
Six blue ghosts
or shuttlecocks
(the hot dogs crew)
missed III and IV
Got It Good
& Together
(time to flip)
palm a keyhole
& a six-eyed tiger
smiles to the center

where a dark eye
rests in primary
sun that's how
i learn to ring
the stop to keep
the weight off

O CAPTAIN, MY
i.m. Chris Doku

      o captain, my
         captain sweatshirt
      is an uncle overboard
      charting
      star garden microdose
across the universe

chris didn't want to go
but he did, & now i don't
want to go to the wake
but will, try to lend a little
smile (awkwardly) behind
this grief & shaggy beard
for (with) my friends'
family, like my friends,
are like family

curious listening
was his philosophy
as captainly advice
stepping off the sea:

"wash yr peepees, boys.
never know
what's gonna happen."
                    he'd say

this is the dumbest poem.
never made claims
to hesiod, let alone cavafy

across the stars
sophocles
was onto something.
all i know is i know
nothing

i should probably
shave.

COUNTY TWANG
for Kevin Kilroy

trusty six-eye river
run the voodoo back
back to my darling
diver, carry me back
& into their heart
the bloody beaten
mouth of a starling

everything is true
everything
as blue is
everything,
as morning
is, & doing
me wrong

you've got me
spinning red
i once became
so unaccustomed
to the detriment
of county twang

if i can find
my get-back
way to oskaloosa
find that ol'
gumball trobairitz

clackity clock
crockery click
lockety hick
robert fripp
that'll be enough

RISK EVERYTHING ON JOY STREET

Joe Cooper grins digging through rare poetry chapbooks in
              downtown antiquarian bookstore

Joe Cooper poses demurely over a crock of lobster Mac

Joe Cooper scowls at the trail gate entrance to snowy Dogtown

Joe Cooper displays young artist's drawing of hamburger
              brought along for the trip

Joe Cooper pulls OG copy of The Kinks' Lola from wall display
              at Mystery Train

Joe Cooper stands thoughtfully before a Rothko in MFA
              exhibition on "Seeking Stillness"

Joe Cooper risks everything in the middle of Joy Street in
              front of brownstone misidentified as John Wieners'
              former home

Joe Cooper poses as a tourist on Gloucester docks beside some
              lobster traps

Joe Cooper disappears into Fort Point proprioception in
              front of a house misidentified as Charles Olson's
              former residence

Where is the person who is in the poem you wrote for him?

Joe Cooper walks his rural Virginia homestead, surveying
        familiar wooded hills in late morning, children by his
        side, infant son strapped to his chest, keeping time.
        To risk is a heartbeat, to risk meal enough to forage for.

Two Sonneteers walk into a bar in heaven:

"When the time of the fearful trip has come…"
"…thus far the miles are measured from thy friends"

SONNET ON BERRIGAN'S BIRTHDAY

Morning's milk pools at the foot of the dumpster
jaunts across driveway, left on Short, continues downhill
in the direction of the flaming trees.
Maybe some will be saved by kind gestures of foolhardy pirates
or well-meaning potato peels. i still baffle & swoon
against the text   butterflies domino against the stars of
your eyelids (elegies). Would you like to leave
a tip for the team? The wise man is only a fool;
Elegant baristas keep the universe well
loved & locked at the buoyant surface of their hearts.
Maybe people need heroes? i am tired of that,
languish on steps of Ruggles Baptist Beacon & Saint Mary's
miss the bus to sip the divine of apocryphal caffeine,
        "alive with borrowed warmth"
Lost in the eye of an early sun, loving them.

SILK DEGREES

holding breath
in a flaming taxi
Boz Scaggs
silently protests
Pluto reinstatement
as a planet   first,
a body needs
establish stable orbit
around the sun
thousands of bodies
meet this condition;
that's to say nothing of
ecliptic perturbations
of the wandering spirit

SOME VELVET MORNING

after Alice Notely

mornings I wonder if I
have enough warm
heartedness to allow
myself to hate the day
with occasional panic
by evenings i wander
with rigor and wonder
what's tomorrow got
that i don't? that i want
and go to, what i won't.
new balance is what
it takes to cross a river
and tansy, tansy, tansy!
i dip my aim, i oar
and row and row
for oblivion's coxswain
(Virgil's pervy heckler)
awash in bitter buttons

11/19

ACROSS THE FULL

every chair's
taken at urgent
care, across the full
beaver moon's
watery runway
alone along
the sliced ecliptic
one red sail
keep finding
the way to
wherever's
land, & lift
& t h a t s
   a wrap

NOVEMBER 20
day after Joanne Kyger's Birthday

"It's been crazy
all these appointments. I
have prescriptions to fill.
They say we can't turn
any walk-ins away.
I guess that's what happens
when decisions get
made by people
at a big company
making millions of dollars
without an idea of what it's
like on the ground."

(Jab, sting)

Assess recipient status
Screen for precautions
Use new sterile needle
for each injection
Cleanse vial stopper
with new sterile alcohol pad
Ensure vaccine amount
in syringe equals 0.3 mL
Administer vaccine immediately
by intramuscular injection
in deltoid muscle

Observe recipients
after for immediate
adverse reaction

the overworked pharmacist

speaks her truth

tell her i appreciate her

wish happy thanksgiving

wait out observation by florist's station

                            in big world supermarket

                    strange to believe
            i was tuning
                        to a milky astral bath of stars
        maybe what it was was just
                            adrenaline gland music
fuzzing over other inner frequencies
            while outside pricks and stings

                                i just want to stay
                        alive
        pick wine-dark flowers for the party

NOVEMBER 21

I wake up 1:07 Sunday morning
muscles sore fever chills head a throbbing cotton ball brain
after much coffee hobo life booster reefer & messy conversation
about the state
of the relationship
preferring I be more "present"
distracted on my phone while we watch teevee
not doing much of anything
(well. that's whole new channel…)
after regretful tones & statements
we agree to gentler acknowledgment
nevertheless, in sheets I blubber fully-clothed,
dreading Sunday family lunch

what echoes out of tiredness
gone down to the skinny
learning about now
is it excuse,
or "reason" ?
we learn to live closer together

with our mistakes   heartaches, set back
to seek rare interlude in pleasure   seek truth

Quiet like a fuse

NOTES

This manuscript was written in my iPhone notes section throughout Scorpio Season (Oct 23— Nov 21, 2021). I'm grateful to the authors of two Instagram posts I regularly referred back to for inspiration throughout the writing:

"Welcome to Scorpio season! Remember who the F you are! Refuse toxic behavior! Make moody playlists! Do sexy brooding! Wear all black everything! Witches! Cast spells for healing! Make magic and emotional mayhem! Life is short! Death is inevitable! Risk everything for joy!"—Chani Nicholas

"It's Scorpio season. Forget small talk. I want to know who hurt you. What are you afraid of? How are you healing? What brings you pleasure? Do you study the esoteric? Do you want to go hang out in a dungeon or a library or both? We're talkin' 50 shades of spirituality here."— Christian B. West

"Pleasure's a fish / & I'm a water sign"— lyric by Digable Planets song "For Corners" on their 1994 album *Blowout Comb.*

"there's no do-overs"— voice message from Michele.

"It will be as much an improvement over Sounds as that was over Summer Days"— album preview for Beach Boys' *Smile* sessions, which were ultimately scrapped.

"inspiring beauty & respect ... are we being our best?"— maybe Whalen?

"All we need is a tragic universe", "chromatically the structure unfolds" and "in either the sensuous or the metaphysical dimension"— from Daniel K.L. Chua and Alexander Rehding's *Alien Listening: Voyager's Golden Record and Music from Earth* (Zone Books, 2021).

"& the sea is a bedtime story" and "to satisfy beyond advantage"— OOPS, forgot to notate the origins of these quotes. Apologies and gratitude to the authors.

Recovering the Jewel from Dragon Palace— erasure of an email blast from a clothing company about women Japanese skin divers.

Heartbreak is behind him but hope is always just ahead, a pin-light through the clouds in the shape of a mythological figure known only as "babe".— Pitchfork review for War on Drugs' album *I Don't Live Here Anymore*

"You can't force something to be your truth" — Co-Star horoscope

"How come you're not movin', Murph? He goes, what did I just tell you?"—Overheard conversation on the streets of Cambridge

"Under Massachusetts' Fallen Tree Law wherever the tree landed, that person is responsible for dealing with it, regardless of where the tree came from."
—Boston Globe Tweet

Devil's Night—Dedicated to Daniel Duhmel a/k/a legendary underground British-American rapper MF DOOM (July 13, 1971— October 31, 2020), who made masks cool before they were.

"are they my forces or the forces I'm within?"
—Joanne Kyger

"It's only life waveing to its self"—Peter Orlovsky

"good night everone / marijhuana"— anonymous note left
on a typewriter at a party at 3020 24th Street, Boulder, CO
in the summer of 2005.

"There is no angry way to say B U B B L E S"
—street advertisement at Downtown Crossing

King Tide—(Maybe) a poet's most important contribution
to society is to become accustomed to rejection. Flawed
Swiftian argument linking global impacts to personal choices
after reading article on kayakers rowing from Boston Harbor
onto Long Wharf Pier on day of astronomically highest tides
of the year, called "king tides".

Sting Catalogue—collage of vocabulary from L.L. Bean's
2021 Winter Catalogue, and quotes from a snowboarding
documentary Michele was watching at the time.

Bus Ride—song title by Canadian electronic music
producer Kaytranada on his debut album *99.9%* (XL
Recordings, 2016).

"Where is the person who is in the poem you wrote for him?"—Jack Spicer, from a poem in *Be Brave to Things: Uncollected Poetry and Plays* (Wesleyan, 2021).

"Maybe people need heroes? I am tired of that."
— Boz Skaggs from a 1978 interview.

"Alive with borrowed warmth"—Ted Berrigan, the poem about borrowing Ron Padgett's car coat

Two Sonneteers—The two sonneteers quoted are Ted Berrigan, and William Shakespeare (natch).

Some Velvet Morning—Title is taken from a song by Lee Hazelwood and grafted into the first line "Mornings I wonder if I…" from Alice Notley's poem "Mornings".

November 20th—Right column is instruction from CDC pamphlet on Pfizer COVID-19 Vaccine Preparation and Administration.

"Quiet Like a Fuse"—Song title from jazz guitarist Julian Lage's album *Squint* (Blue Note, 2021).

ACKNOWLEDGMENTS

Many thanks to the editors of the small lit journals who published some of these poems in earlier versions:

Juliet Cook for publishing "Video Voice" in the December issue of *Thirteen Myna Birds*.

Barracuda Guarisco at Really Serious Lit for publishing "'81 / 2 or so..." as part of RSL's Disappearing Chapbook series publication *Star Chart*.

Much love to my friends and family, and especially Michele, who inspires me to no end with her patience, understanding, and support.

ANDREW K. PETERSON is a poet and editor. He is the author of five poetry books, most recently *A Blue Nocturne Notebook* (Spuyten Duyvil, 2021), and *Three-Way Street*, a collaborative correspondence with Jared Hayes and Reed Bye (Turnsol Editions, 2020). His 2017 chapbook *The Big Game Is Every Night* was mailed to the White House alongside other publications from Moria Books' Locofo Chaps series as collective protest. A previous chapbook *bonjour meriwether and the rabid maps* (Fact-Simile Press, 2011) was featured in an exhibition on poets' maps at the University of Arizona's Poetry Center. In 2017 he was a co-organizer of the Boston Poetry Marathon. He is a cofounding editor of the literary journal *summer stock*, and lives in Boston.

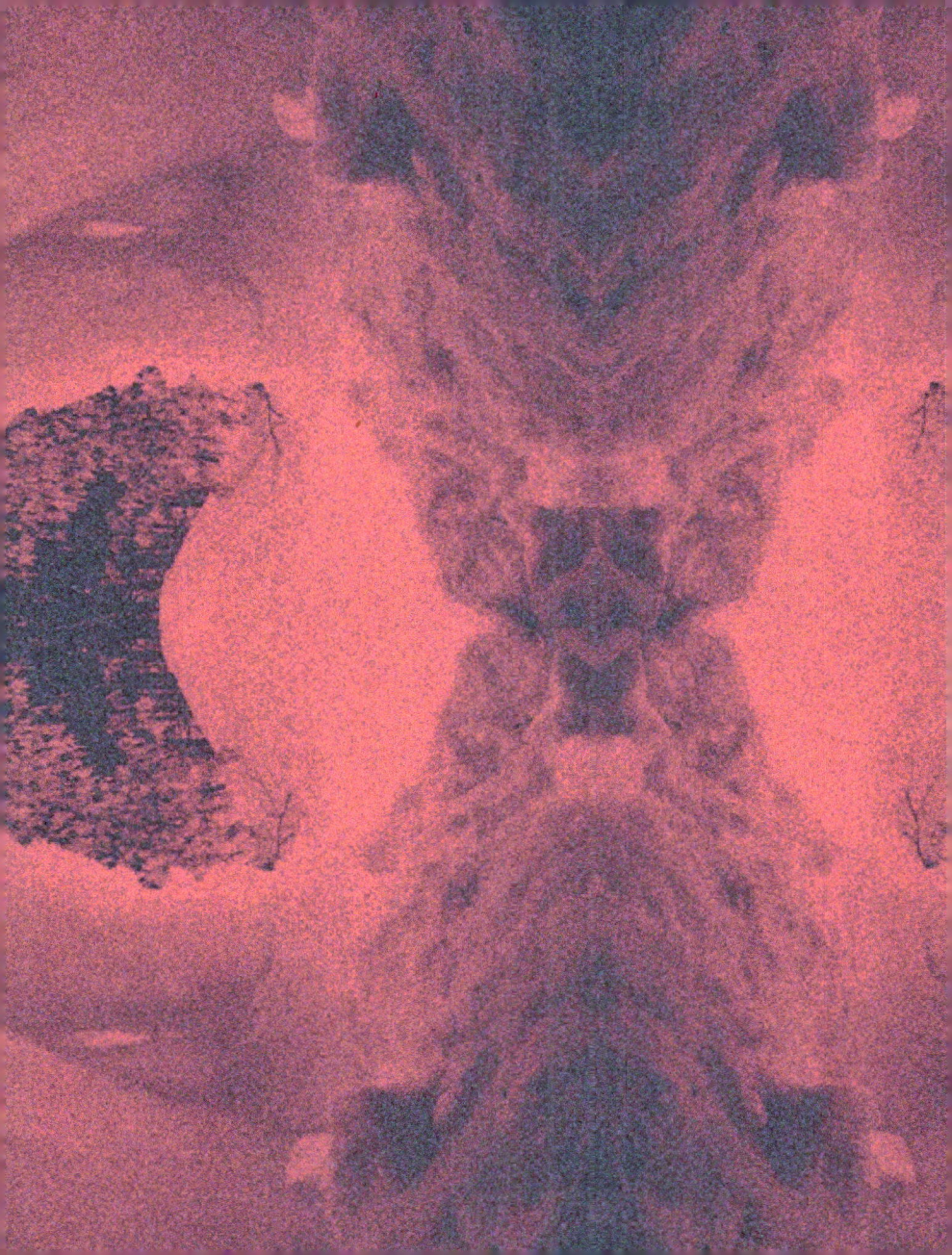

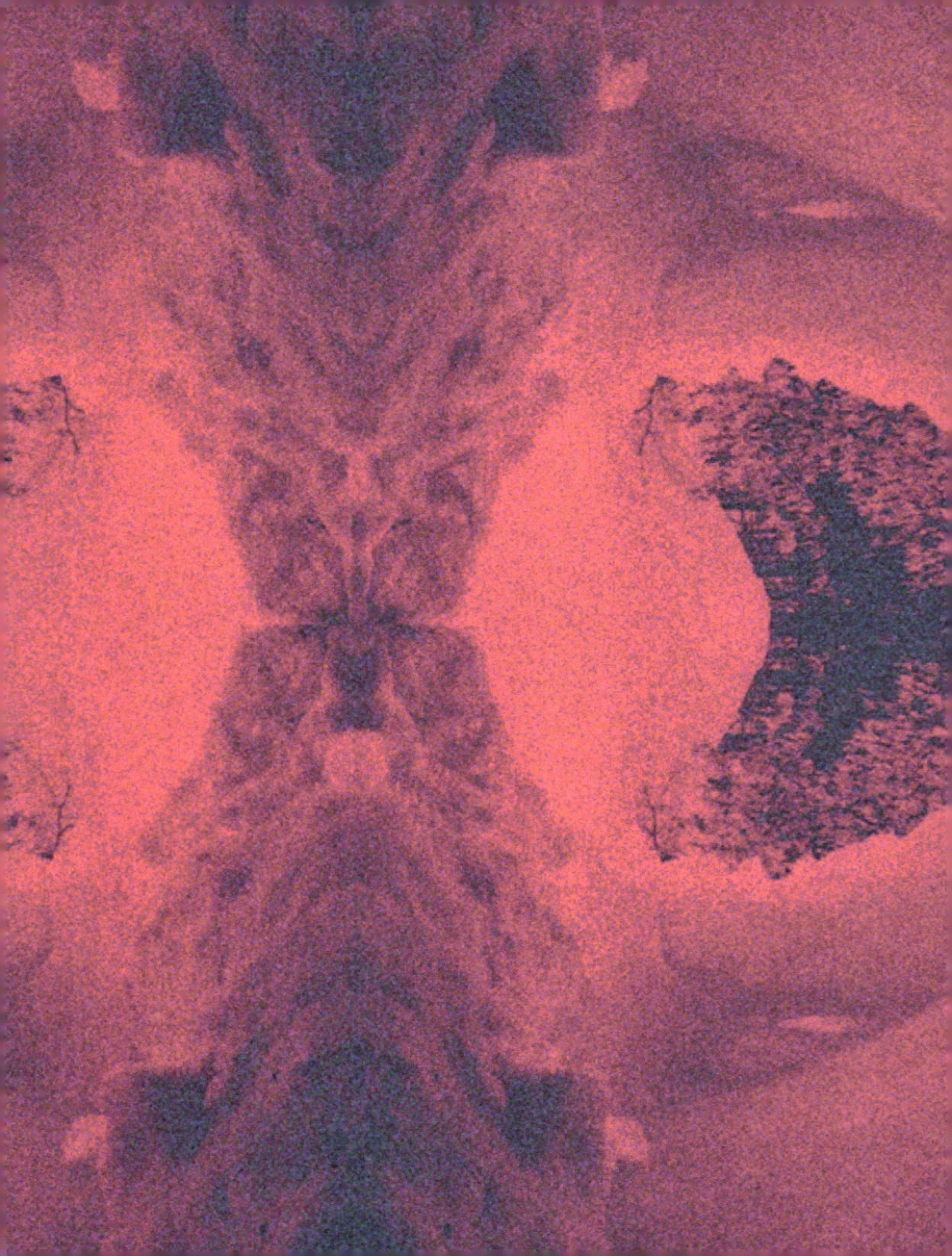